Success in Higl

Achieving the mindset to be a winner throughout life

Introduction

Hi, my name is Ben. This book has been years in the making—really, I've been wanting to write the ideas and thoughts and concepts contained within this work for years, ever since I graduated High School. The reason is because my high school experience had a lot of ups and downs, and after meeting a TON of people who've had the same or similar experience during their high school careers, I decided that this book and its concepts MUST be written and put out to the public so that other people don't have to go through what I've been through myself. It's only normal to have a roller-coaster ride during the high school years; as a teenager you go through a bunch of transitions, both physically and mentally, and it is within this short time span (I know a lot of you guys think "oh my gosh, it's SOOOO long, graduation seems like it'll never come!", I felt the same way!) that you truly shape your life and how you will be for the REST of your existence on this planet. Therefore, I believe that in order to maximize your success in life (however you define success for yourself to be), the proper mindset must be adopted, and this is the best time in your life to do it.

We see a ton of people go through life without achieving success, not because they don't want to be successful (although many people think this without knowing it), rather because they don't know HOW to do it, and this is extremely frustrating, not knowing WHAT the formula is. One way to get this knowledge is to read as much as you can, as this will expose you to ideas that would take you years or decades to figure out yourself. Knowledge really is power. But that just tells you how to do things, techniques and ideas. The other component, the one that will truly define your outcome whether you are successful or not, whether you are able to implement the tactics that you read about, is your <u>mindset</u>.

You see, mindset is everything. Based on what your perspective is, that's what will determine your actions. Mindset can be defined as your perspective, your outlook, your opinions on things, etc.

A great example of this: if you think that a certain person is a bad person, then even when he does something good you will believe that he is really doing the good act because he has some evil plan behind it. Another example: if, in your mind, you think that it's so hard to get an A on a test, I guarantee you'll have a much greater difficulty in achieving that A. Not because it is more difficult, but because of the way that you think, you'll unconsciously *make* things more difficult for yourself.

That is the goal of this book, to alter your mindset so that you can start thinking about life in the ways that you need to in order to be successful.

Yes, there are people out there who also write self-improvement books as well, but what I've realized is that most of the time, if not ALL of the time, they are looking to "change lives", i.e. to shape up lives that are currently fractured, and many of them do so wonderfully. But they are looking to change lives because that's what they know how to do, as they themselves changed their own lives after a very rough start.

My goal in this book and much after it is not to *change* lives that are already broken, rather it is to create lives, to educate the young members of society in the incubator of the school system on how to have a winning mindset and perspective, so that they don't experience that "rough start" in the first place. "Begin at the source, change the outcome".

Even though our personalities are formed when we are just babies, i.e. whether or not we are outgoing people, whether or not we enjoy taking risks, etc., during the formative years of high school is when we shape our habits and our mindsets, when we are the most vulnerable, or in a more positive language, the most impressionable that we will EVER be in our entire lifespan. We hear ideas, and we adapt those ways of thinking and those opinions that integrate the smoothest with the ideas and opinions that we were exposed to while growing up, and previous experiences that we had up until this point.

In a sense, you can say that we are formed at the base layer when we are very young children, and then as teenagers we improve upon them and solidify that foundation. For example, a guy in high school will say that he's a Democrat, even though he doesn't really know the positions and opinions of that point of view, even though neither of his parents are at all involved with politics, rather because the views that were believed in his home and amongst his family members during his younger years matched the views of that political party, therefore he most associates himself with the Democratic Party, because that's what he *already believed in*; he's just associating himself with something that shares his views. We form the notions that will carry us throughout the rest of our lives, and the mindsets that WILL determine whether or not we are successful (unless we take tremendous efforts later on to change that), during the years that we are in high school.

This is why I wrote this specifically for people of high school age. Although there will for sure be value to the reader who has already passed this stage of life, I feel it's important to focus on this group more than others.

Ready for the ride?

Chapter 1: Positivity

Let's talk a bit about positivity, as this is the most important part of being successful, because, as we just said, your mindset <u>is the ONLY thing that holds you back from *anything*, since it determines the actions that you are going to take</u>. If your mind is always thinking of negative thoughts, things like "I can't do this", "that's never going to happen", and even things like "I'm feeling terrible today", that will impact the way you perform in life.

Try this now: think in your head how you feel sick. Really, think about it, focus on it long enough, and you'll start to *feel* sick! Now try it the other way: think and imagine in your head that you are the BEST person in the world, and that you can accomplish ANYTHING. Doesn't that make you feel better? Or try thinking about a vacation in Miami for a whole month straight; I assure you that your desire to go there will increase each day.

So let's get you on track to being the most positive that you can be in your life, and feeling better about yourself and what you can accomplish. I actually recently heard of a study that was done that showed that our minds are 31% more efficient when we have a positive outlook than if we have a negative one. In order to start this change, you have to realize that there is positivity in the world, and there is negativity too. Let's define both of them right now. Positivity is the mindset, the outlook on life that is always seeing how things *could* be done, how things *will* get better, and how the world *is* a great place; it's the state of mind that sees everything as good; this will move you forward in life. Negativity is the exact opposite: negativity is all about things being bad—how people are cheap, how the neighborhood is terrible, how the weather is always bad, etc.; this will keep you where you are in life, it will "put the brakes on" to your advancement.

Think about it: how can you *ever* get ahead in life if you're just thinking "can't/won't/impossible/not happening/bad/etc."? That's just a recipe for inaction, and nobody achieves any measure of success by not doing anything! People achieve success by saying things like "I'll get it done" and "let's figure it out" and "I'm doing amazing today!", because that type of mindset is very forward-moving; a negative mindset is constricting and keeps people in their place.

As you become a more positive person by working on your attitude you will become more attuned to what positivity is, which people are positive, etc., and realize that those people and things that you once thought were positive are actually very negative, and you just didn't realize it because you were very negative yourself. "It takes one to know one" as they say, and the same goes for positivity as well.

How do you become more positive? In order to understand what the process is, we need to build the foundation, that's something I'm very into, because if you don't have the foundation—the inherent understanding as to the WHY—then even if you do somehow figure out the HOW, it won't last, because your understanding will be deficient.

Okay, here's the kicker: <u>your mindset is determined by the things that you put into your mind, every influence that you expose your mind to</u>. Based on the thoughts and ideas that you put into your mind will determine EVERYTHING in your life: how you feel, the things that you tell yourself, how you perform (ever heard the term "winning mindset"?), etc. EVERYTHING is about your mindset.

So let's get you on the road to being positive and having a winning outlook! The first step is to write down all the things that influence your mind, things that go into your head. This includes music, TV, apps on your phone, games, friends, people, news, the colors of your walls, *everything*! Write these down now:

_____

_____

_____

_____

_____

_____

_____

_____

_____

_____

If you aren't able to fill in all of the lines, don't worry, you will become more aware of everything that influences you as you go throughout your day. Now see which of these things contribute to your being more positive, and which things actually influence you to be more negative/don't feel good about yourself/sad/hopeless/etc., and then cut those things from your life: books, people, movies, TV, etc., because all of these things do not contribute to your moving forward in life one bit. Your mind is the most valuable and private thing that you have in this world, you must do whatever it takes to protect it.

Also, when I talk about cutting out everything negative from your life, I did not mean to just walk away from people who are negative, because I believe that people should deal with problems in life and try to solve them, rather than just running away from them. But sometimes it *is* necessary to do so. In other words, if you want them to still be in your life (they are important to you, or they have something they can contribute to your advancement) you have to confront them and say "listen, I really appreciate you for the value that you bring into my life, but if you want to remain in my circle you'll have to change your attitude to be more positive". Then help them be more positive, share the tips and the process that I gave you above for identifying negative influences and content with them and *help* them! But if the person/people aren't willing to change, you have to cut them from your surroundings, you cannot afford to affect your mind with negative thoughts and ideas as they will only hold you back.

Now it may be hard for some people to change, but realize this: first of all, we were all born positive—all babies smile as a natural instinct, and once they are able to express themselves they have an extremely positive, upbeat attitude on life, an attitude which must be maintained and protected like gold (because it *will* get you the gold!), or else it will be compressed and withheld and shrunk by the influences of society. So it *is* possible to change back. The more influenced we have been by negative societal influences around us, the harder it will be to revert back to the "childish" positivity that we were meant to have[1].

Secondly, with regards to picking your friends: just like when you're buying a stock, or joining a company, or pretty much anything that you invest your time or energy into, the most important thing for it to be is that it's growing (even if there *are* dips every now and then) so too when picking people to surround you—they can have fallings here or there—they're people, they're not perfect—but they *must* have growth at the end of the day, or else they will just hold you down from reaching your true potential.

It's also good to know that a positive attitude will always win over negative ones, you will always be that "shining light" in the room (and your smile will radiate that!), while others are perceived as mere black holes. People will admire and respect

---

[1] As a side note with regards to positive/negative influences, look at movie posters or the front cover of a DVD case. Did you ever realize that most of the time, the expressions of the actors on the front of the "grown-up" movies are more stern, serious, angry, emotionless, etc., while the expressions of the actors on the front of a kids movie are more upbeat and happy?

you for your "can-do" outlook on life, and you will get more friends as a result as well, as people will be more attracted to you (come on, no one wants to introduce themselves to that guy in the room who looks like he's angry at everyone!). Don't be afraid to always smile; yes, there are "interesting" people who smile constantly, but people know that they are mentally deficient; your smile should be backed by that intelligent look in your eyes, and by how you act.

And people's resistance will melt in your path when you show a smile: I remember once in high school, a teacher who was honestly a bit kooky was once walking towards me and a group of guys, and as he passed us he gave each one of us a big smile and said "good morning! How are you today!". I thought it was weird when he was doing that to the other guys around me, but once he looked me in the eye and wished me a good morning as well, I don't know what it was, but something made me think "you know, he's really friendly and he always appears positive".

That's human nature, we are naturally attracted to people who smile and favor them more than others who don't. A great example is a baby—people LOVE babies and will go out of their way to please them! Your smile will be one of the most powerful negotiating/influencing tools that you will ever use in your life.

Chapter 2: Life is NOT hard

When I was in high school and in college, I pretty much always got B's. It was a B+ this test, a B the next, and occasionally I got an A here or there. Why? Because of my mindset: I thought that the only reason I'd be able to snag that A would be if it was easy, and "life is not easy", right? That's what so many people told me about virtually everything. This caused me to make things unnecessarily hard for myself—I was under the impression that tests were *supposed* to be hard, and therefore I thought I had to study a TON in order to have any hopes of doing well, and if I ever saw a question that I knew the answer to I'd think "wait a second...this must be more complex than I thought it was when I first read it...let me go over it again".

That didn't really help me: I over-studied, and as a result I never really understood the information, I only memorized my notes, and therefore my grades were not as good as some of my peers. This is one thing that a lot of people get wrong: <u>life is not hard</u>! Life is actually very EASY, but most people don't have the right attitude to realize this, they just don't have the positive mindset that they need to in order to believe this idea.

Let me ask you a question: is life hard for an animal, something that does not contain the brain capacity to build buildings, to think of even the most rudimentary philosophical idea, or even add a few numbers together? NO! Of course it's not, because they just work out of instinct, they just do <u>whatever makes sense</u> for them to do at that particular moment. So too, life for us is actually something that is easy; we are actually built to have certain instincts that compel us to do what is right in life, the problem is that most of us complicate life with all of our little calculations and stuff. Don't make life hard for yourself, you are great, and have the ability to do great things too. Stay positive!

Let's talk a bit more about this concept of "life is easy". It is NOT meant to give you the idea that you should never do anything hard in life, or else you would never accomplish anything incredible. For whenever we push ourselves to do that which is difficult, we move beyond the realm of just being an animalistic being, and enter the realm of extraordinary possibilities. In fact, one of my "targets" every single day, something that I MUST do that day, is that I shoot to do at least 6 things that are either hard or uncomfortable for me to do. Things like calling someone who's business I want who has blown me off and been very rude to me in the past. Saying "I'm sorry" to someone who I've wronged. Going somewhere I know I should go when I don't feel like going there, e.g. the gym. Some days I do NOT want to go swim in the pool for exercise, but every single time that I overcome my desire to just kick back and relax, on those days I feel the best after swimming. You can't grow, not as a person and not in business, if you don't do things that are hard and uncomfortable for you to do, because then you will never have discovered or developed the skills to deal with issues and challenges that are bound to occur.

That's the key: don't make life hard for yourself. A large reason as to why so many people do this is because they have these preconceived notions, these beliefs from when they were younger that they've been "educated" with about how life is a lot of work. For instance: getting a great job. Most people think that you have to send your resume to a hundred different places in order to land that job, but in reality, all you're doing there is playing a numbers game. It's really much easier than that: you just find a few people that you'd be willing to work for, and call them up. If you have a friend who already works for that person, the job is basically yours (getting ahead in life really IS all about WHO you know, and not WHAT you know, more on that later).

Another example is studying for a test: most people think that you need to study HARD, that you need to review the material again and again and again. In reality you don't—if you study *smart* and work on *understanding* the information instead of just memorizing it, it's so much easier. In fact, when I was in college I was going over material around 12 times before each test. Then I came across a method of studying and taking notes (howtostudyincollege.com), and all of a sudden I had 6 more hours a week of free time, *and* my grades went up! It's all about working smart, not hard. The hard worker makes $12/hour vacuuming floors, the smart worker buys a Roomba to do the vacuuming for him at $12/hr, and gets paid an additional $12/hr for cleaning the windows too. The point is that life is not as hard as people make it seem, and you'll know for sure that this is true when you start looking at how things might be able to be easier, and implement those ideas into your life.

When I was younger, and even now, I hear people describe things, from jobs to being a parent to just waking up in the morning: "it's sooo hard"! So what?!?! Just because something is hard doesn't mean you shouldn't do it! Some of the best things in life were only attainable for me because they were hard for me to do; I had to *push myself* beyond what I felt comfortable doing in order to get those results! This actually brings me to a most interesting observation: you know how it seems like, in all the stories we read, from fantasies such as Harry Potter all the way to real-life stories about people like Tai Lopez and Grant Cardone, just to name a few, the people with the MAJOR successes, the people who score the highest, are the people who started from nothing? Why is that? I always wondered this, until it hit me: the people who started out with money may have been successful, but they didn't have to push that hard to make their successes a reality. But the ones who started from nothing were the guys who had to push SO HARD in order to even get their foot in the door, and once they started pushing at those incredibly high levels, levels MUCH higher than those that the born-rich were pushing at, they made that discipline part of who they are, and they kept on pushing at those ultra-high levels for the rest of their lives; that was the standard.

And let's say that you aren't starting from absolutely nothing like a lot of these guys were (doing drugs and being completely broke, or sleeping on the floor in the back of a trailer, etc.), how do you begin pushing at those incredibly high levels? The truth is, a guy once told me, you don't have to be like that in order to hit "rock-bottom", because everyone has their own "rock-bottom". For some guys it's being $50,000 in debt, doing drugs, and living on the streets, flipping burgers at a fast-food restaurant making $8/hr. For other people, it may be having only $30,000 in the bank, and making $40,000 a year, but they realize exactly how little money that is, and they see others succeeding and realize that they are at the "rock-bottom" of their potential. And for others it may be the fact that they've woken up late the past 3 days, they're addicted to coffee, and they just got a flat tire.

You see? The people in all of these scenarios are at the bottom of their potential, they only need to realize that, get angry and HATE the position that they're in right now, realize how much they could achieve, and start doing things to get on that road. <u>You create your own "rock-bottom"</u>, and if you want to begin growing right now, look at people more successful than you and realize that you *are* all the way on the bottom right now, and start growing. This is why having good friends (even only 1 or 2) is so important; you don't need to be the most popular guy or girl in your class, but you DO need to have 1 or 2 or a few close friends who can tell you how great you are. Honestly—not just to flatter you.

As the saying goes: "woe to the man who does not know his faults, even more woe to that man who does not know his strengths". You need to realize your potential, and if you don't see what your potential can be, make it up! But think BIG, don't make your potential small. "Shoot for the Moon—even if you miss, you will land among the stars".

Chapter 3: Self-honesty

Okay, up until now we've spoken about the importance of being positive, about the fact that many people make life seem hard when it really isn't, about how you should do those things that appear hard in order to advance in leaps and bounds through life, and now I want to speak about the concept of being honest with yourself. This is an activity that, through my observations, I have realized that very few people do. Most people aren't honest with themselves about who they really are, the things they are good at and the things that they aren't good at, their goals, their self-image, who their friends are…the list goes on and on. I believe that when a person is introspective, in other words he has this awareness of himself and who he is and what he is doing at the present moment, he is able to be honest with himself much more than the people who just get dragged through life by others, and not many people take the few minutes alone by themselves that self-awareness requires.

If you aren't honest with yourself, you may find yourself pursuing a career that you really don't want to do, a person who you don't actually want to be friends with, and making decisions that you don't actually want to make. All it takes is for you to listen to the questions that you are asking yourself ("is this really right for me?", "do I really want to do this?", etc.) and answer them; most people ignore the questions in the first place and then go on a path that they really don't want to go on. There is this saying out there that you should "go with your gut". This is really important and will help you be honest with yourself and your feelings, as your gut feeling can help you determine whether or not what you are doing is the right thing to do; it's our minds picking up on small details that we may not aware of. For instance, I'm sure you can think of someone you don't like, but when I ask you why you don't like them, you tell me that you can't put a finger on why, you just know. Be honest with yourself and you'll see the way life is supposed to be as opposed to the way that you may think it is.

Chapter 4: The Successful Mind

Here is another SUPER IMPORTANT rule in life that you should NEVER violate if you want ANY measure of success in your life at all: NEVER EVER EVER EVER EVER EVER EVER EVER EVER speak badly or make fun of people who are successful!!!!! No matter what they're successful in, be it money, relationships, giving to charity, etc., if you ridicule them, how can you ever expect to achieve success? This includes things that they say, said do, or did. This is something which is so often violated, and this is what holds many people on this planet back from achieving success. Yes, it may be funny, but watching shows like Saturday Night Live which make fun of successful people by either impersonating them, making jokes about them, etc. are so destructive.

STAY AWAY from ANYTHING and EVERYTHING that makes even the slightest joke about someone who is successful. Whether that person is successful in business, in politics, in his career, this is a rule that must NOT be violated. Even if the person is the President of the United States, someone who is tremendously in the public eye espousing his views and opinions to the masses, you can disagree with him on his views, that's okay, but DO NOT, DO NOT, DO NOT make even the slightest joke about him.

Think about it: how can YOU ever have 60 billion dollars if you don't respect the people that do? It is human nature to not emulate the people who we reject in our minds, be aware of that. If you want to become successful, you MUST emulate those who are. Pick a person, or 3 people at the maximum who you aspire to be like, and read/watch EVERYTHING on them, start inculcating their views and opinions into who YOU are, and I guarantee you, your life will change for the better.

Now a lot of people show disrespect toward successful people, mostly towards people who have a ton of money, because they claim that those rich people are snobs and feel entitled, and that's not right of them to act like that, because they are people just like the rest of us. This claim is rooted in jealousy. Realize that, whenever you become jealous of someone you are really being jealous of the fact that you know that you can do that or have that too, but aren't acting at that level of activity just yet. I agree that they are people, and shouldn't lord themselves like dictators over others, but why aren't they entitled?

Think of Bill Gates: yes, when he stays in a hotel he should pay for his stay, but if he would say "listen, your entire business wouldn't be here if not for me, because I created the software that runs all of your marketing, all of your financials, every single operation that is a component of your business, so show me some gratitude and let me stay here for free", yes, that would show a lack of character because he is *asking* of others to respect him, but of course he's entitled! Or how about if the Wright brothers, the people who *invented* airplanes, asked for that? Or how about if the person who pays the most taxes in the city asks for a favor? Yes, *demanding* that others should respect you displays a lack of character, but if they ask with good manners, <u>you</u> would be the snob for not agreeing to show them that reciprocation!

I do agree, however, that there *are* people who are successful and are not pleasant people. But it should still be noted: money is a "magnifier", it only increases that which is already there in the person's personality. So if you see a person who is rich with money and a jerk, I can almost guarantee you that he was a jerk before he made his money! We can see this on the flip-side as well: the people who give the most money away were generous *before* they made their billions, too!

Did you ever stop to think: maybe society only sees rich people as being bad or evil or snobbish because of one of three possible reasons: 1) the people who view them that way are jealous of the rich people (because they realize that they themselves have the potential to get rich too and are just not using their capabilities to the fullest), 2) the rich people were bad people *before* they even had any money (see above), or 3) the rich people were pleasant-mannered people, but once they started getting all this hate and disregard from others, that left a bad taste in their mouth. How would *you* feel if wherever you went, people looked at you with disdain? So I would strongly argue that most rich people are NOT bad people, it's just the negative view that society pushes upon them that brainwashes all of us to think like that, or for them to act according to how society perceives them. Come on, let's see the TRUTH and be successful ourselves!

Let me give you an example of what I mean: in Maryland, where I currently live, there is a city called Chevy Chase, which is one of the richest cities in all of America. Now a lot of people complain about how high tax rates are (this is normal and has been going on in societies for thousands of years), but what they don't realize is that yes, they may be paying a lot for taxes, but that's only relative; the people in Chevy Chase are probably paying as much money in taxes as half of the entire state combined! Why would I show any disdain for someone who gives up so much money to make my stay in this state a better one? Even if you don't agree with this, at the very least, RESPECT those who have money and or success, NO MATER WHAT (even if they *do* appear as snobs/cold people, because you can always find something positive about anyone), because if you don't respect success, you will NEVER be successful yourself. That's a guarantee.

Chapter 5: Your Decision

This leads me to another super-important point: kind of like what I said before, that everything that you do in life is determined by your mindset, a <u>huge thing</u> that will determine whether or not you are successful in life is your decision that you make. You see, everyone makes a decision in life, one way or another. Some people decide to be successful, and others say "I don't need that", and proceed to live an average life. But the truth is that you NEED to be successful, you NEED to make a difference! You need success because you need to help others who don't have the mindset to be successful themselves. You need success because you weren't born to be a beggar. You need success because it's easier to be successful than it is to fail. You need to be successful so that you don't just live your life as a pawn of other people, rather you live the life that YOU want on YOUR terms.

Many people believe in "equality", I'm not sure why though, as it doesn't even exist. There will ALWAYS be a winner and a loser in this world, no matter what, that's just the way the world is. No two people are equal. You have to decide right now: are you going to be a winner, and live the life that you deserve? Or are you going to be a loser, and live the life that other people want you to live so that *they* can live the lives that they deserve?

You know, even as I write this, it kills me to know that, in light of that line that I wrote above "If you don't want to be like the 1% (the successful), don't do what the 99% of people do", so many people actually know how to be successful, they just either don't take the first step that they need to in order to get on the road, or they aren't honest with themselves and think that they are okay, that everything will be all right with them. Because that's just the way people are. The reason why the quote says to not do the things that the 99% *do*, and it doesn't say not to *think* the way the 99% of people *think*, is because in truth, a lot of people know what is best for them, what the right things are to do, yet they don't actually take the action to even get the ball rolling in the right direction. So even though I'm writing this to inspire people, I'm afraid that only around 20% of the people will actualize the information in this book into their lives and will change for the better, around 40% will say "that's good information", and then implement only one or two of the concepts, and the other 40% will say "that's good stuff", and then never do anything with it.

But go ahead, prove me wrong. And even if I'm right, please, please, please be part of that 20%, it's the only thing that's worthwhile to do, to get out of the mess of misinformation that everyone else is stuck in, and make life exceptional for yourself!

Chapter 6: Your "Escape"

There's a concept that I believe is <u>so critical</u> for being successful that I found out while I was in college. In order to understand it I'll have to lay the foundational understanding first. There are two things that you must understand: firstly, every single human on this planet must be obsessed with *something*. We are born to be obsessed; when a baby gets a toy in his hand, he is completely focused on just that toy, and is completely oblivious to everything else around him. That's just part of human nature, we have certain things that we are "in to". These things many times, if not all the time, are determined by the influences we had as a young child—things our parents gave to us, or ideas that they educated us with. As an example, my father always ridiculed "pop culture" toys such as Power Rangers, Sesame Street, Barbies, etc. because "they just want your money". As a result, I was never into those things myself, because as children we all want to be like our parents (even if we don't later on, and that's normal and healthy to be like that). But instead I was obsessed with fantasy and sci-fi things, because that's what my father was into and thought was really cool.

Second, here's a little story about what I learned while doing Physics homework while in college:

Throughout my college career, I was always known to be one of the most diligent students, the hardest studier. While others had their phones next to their textbooks and took breaks every 30 minutes to walk around and talk, I would be able to go hours at a time doing work and studying without getting distracted. Now in the summer I took a Physics course, very hard for me, because I'm not that good at math (or at least I didn't think I was). A family member, wanting to help me study better, shared with me an article that said that it's been proven that the most effective way of studying and retaining information was to take a 15-minute break every 51 minutes, because people's attention spans can't withstand focusing longer than that. All of a sudden I started becoming like the masses. When I looked at my watch and saw that the clock was nearing 51 minutes, my brain started shutting down. Mindset is key. I *thought*, I actually *believed* that I couldn't absorb anything past 51 minutes, and that I *had* to take a break. So I started to play Angry Birds on my phone for around 15 minutes every 51-minute interval. After a couple intervals I realized that I started feeling the need to take a break and play every 30 minutes or so. Then I learned a super-important lesson: the more that you take a break, the more you *have* to take a break.

This is a lesson that goes for taking breaks, for going on vacations, or anything that distracts you from the normal day-to-day schedule. Why? Because since you're thinking of that vacation in Florida so much, that *want* turns into a *need*; your desire becomes so strong it's nearly impossible to resist.

Let's recap for a second: #1: we *must* and are *going* to be obsessed with something; #2: the more you do something, the more you *have* to do it.

And now for the real gold: I learned that you can reprogram your mind to become obsessed with *whatever you choose,* all you need to do is start doing it more frequently so that you start *having* to do it more. Like, everyone has an "outlet", a hobby, right? Here's an example of how to reprogram that: let's say right now your hobby is flying remote-controlled helicopters, or something. But you want to make some money, either at a job, or as a "side-hustle". What you actually do is *reprogram* your brain: let's say that you want to make money by selling stuff on eBay. The next time that you feel like you need a break, instead of flying that helicopter, list a few things on eBay. Yes, it's gonna be a bit difficult at first, because you're "going against the grain" of what you're used to, but after a while, selling stuff on eBay will *become* your "outlet".

It's scary, and really cool, and it works SO well.

On that note, I am going to tell you something else that is absolutely critical for your success, both in high school, and when you are in your 20s, in your 30s, and beyond. Pay attention. During this critical period in your life you are defining what you will become in the future as a person, and you are defining your activities as well. That doesn't mean to say that you can't change in the future, but when you're a teenager you're really planting things inside yourself, and it takes a lot of time and energy to change the habits later on that you will become accustomed to doing while you are in this timeframe.

Now let's get real: one of the things that you will define right now is that <u>whenever you're down, there *is* an activity that you do to relax/escape</u>. For me it was playing guitar and selling things on eBay. The reason why these activities are so important in your life is because in the future, no matter what age you are, you *will* revert to these activities whenever you're feeling down. It's how we escape. It's normal.

However, many kids out there take on habits that are destructive to themselves and others in order to escape, because the whole principal behind the escape is that it has to be something that makes you feel good (because right now you're feeling bad/down for whatever reason). This is why a lot of people fall to drugs, and that's one of the worst escapes, because it's not just an escape activity, it's also chemicals that you are artificially putting into your brain to make you feel good, which will make it harder for you to feel good about yourself without the drugs. Others escape by doing activities such as playing video games or listening to music. However, the best escapes are the ones that make you money, and that's true for two reasons: 1) when you're older and feeling down about yourself, a lot of the time the problem that you're dealing with can be fixed with money (not being able to pay the bills, getting into a car accident, not being able to afford the fancy cars that all your friends are driving, etc.), and 2) it's production, and people feel good about themselves when they are producing something, getting fruits for their efforts.

You really have to rate all the activities that you can think of to escape with: the ones that make you money would be high on the scale, doing something creative such as painting or playing a musical instrument would be in the middle, because it has the probability of making you money (selling your art, music, performing, etc.), and things which hurt yourself such as eating, doing drugs, drinking, going to places you shouldn't be going to are all the way on the bottom.

This is key: while you're in high school, while your mind is still in "flexible mode", get involved in something that you can do that makes money, whether it be mowing a lawn, teaching someone how to get fit, or anything else that makes money, and even if you can't think of how this activity can possibly make you feel relaxed and good about yourself, don't worry, after you've mowed a few lawns or mopped a few floors you'll realize it's very relaxing, and you'll feel great about yourself having that extra cash in your pocket at the end of the day.

Chapter 7: Money Mindset

There's a misconception out there that I hinted to in the previous piece: that "money can't buy everything" and that "money can't solve all your problems". While these statements are true, they are usually meant to instill within the members of society that money is not something important and not something worth pursuing, and that you should focus on more "wholesome" things, such as spending time with your family, reading books to gain knowledge about things, or gazing up at the stars at night, just enjoying the beauty of nature. While I agree that "wholesome" things are activities that we should all participate in, I strongly discourage this mindset that "money isn't important". After all, it *is* important, I mean, you can't survive on this planet without it.

People also say "money won't solve all your problems", but they don't realize the rest of that statement: "but it *can* solve *most* of your problems!". People who make that statement are usually coming from one of two areas: 1) they already have money, and they realize that it *won't* solve their marriage, their child-rearing problems, get them more friends, etc., and they thought it would; 2) they don't have any money and have given up on trying to get it in quantities great enough to help themselves. And it's true—most of the problems that people experience in life can be solved with money; whether you like it or not, money *does* make living a lot better.

A lot of schoolteachers I know promote this idea that money is not a good thing, that money makes people evil, and that there should be a disdain for people who have more money than the rest of us. Refer to what I wrote earlier on this topic about defaming people with money, but the fact is that money is a needed thing and should NOT be looked at as something disgusting. The only people who think that money isn't important are the people who don't have any money to begin with! The next time you meet someone who has millions of dollars, ask him if money is important or not. I have even had people tell me "I don't like money" because they're scared of it. Hey, you're not scared of money, you're scared of what you might *do* with it because you don't know how to be <u>responsible</u> with it! It's yourself you don't trust, not your money! Get real!

One of my biggest fears (and a reality that I've been noticing) is to be 70 years old and not have any money. I see *way* too many people in my community who have gray hair, and whose clothes are bedraggled and torn, and who still drive their car from 20 years ago that's missing half the steering wheel because at one point they realized that they don't have too much time left and they've got to live on whatever money they have in the bank account, and (oops!) they forgot to factor in the unexpected (medical issues, car accidents, etc.).

This is also the reason why you see people in the grocery store paying with cash, people cutting up credit cards, etc. because they think that the credit cards are the problem. It's not the cards, it's your discipline! It's not so much about *making* a budget than it is about *sticking* to one! Money is not evil, it's a misconception that people have because they occasionally see money being used for evil things, and they see people go into $80,000 worth of credit card debt because they can't control their spending. The real problem by the way, is not the spending, it's the fact that they don't have enough income to satisfy their spending needs. This is one of the things that you gain in school by going for the good grades: aside from the fact that it helps you cultivate the mindset that greatness and being the TOP are achievable, it also instills within you the quality of discipline, because you have to give certain things up in order to get those good grades.

Here's the rule: if you want anything great in life, you will HAVE to give certain things up. Now don't take that too literally and just give up on every little thing, rather realize that the things that you'll have to give up are <u>small comforts</u> which will be worthwhile to give up relative to the comforts and freedom that you can and will achieve when you become successful. For example: give up playing video games for 2 hours each day and work 2 hours more so that one day you can be playing video games (on better technology, by the way) the *entire* day, and not have to worry about where your money is going to come from.

Along the same lines is the fact that in order to achieve success you must begin to take responsibility for EVERYTHING in your life. Like we said before, don't do what the masses do, we're trying to put you ahead of the game here. Most people watch TV, listen to what the Government is doing, and then blame everyone for their bad situation. What do you expect? If you're being convinced on TV that the Government or some other outside source is responsible for your situation, it's very hard not to accept that. But the reality is: YOU are responsible for everything that happens to you. Even if you're not, what I want you to do, starting right now, is to start taking responsibility for it, because then you will make it a habit to do so. The reason why this is so important when going for success is because <u>you can only change what you can control</u>. For example, you cannot change the flight path of that airplane up 30,000 feet in the sky when you're just a spectator down on the ground. But get into the cockpit of that plane and you can determine where it's going to go.

Now if you're thinking right now: "but I don't want to become a control freak", I totally understand, that's another misconception that society has tried to tame everyone down with. Why don't you want to be in control? The only person who is labeled a "control freak" is either the perfectionist who wants to do the job of 1,000 people all by himself, or the person who controls people with anger and doesn't lead them properly. All great leaders control their following, but none of them would be labeled as "control freaks", right? Martin Luther King Jr., Mahatma Gandhi, Abraham Lincoln were all great leaders, but they didn't control their followers in a bad or cruel way, right. Be in control of everything, take the wheel of your life, don't just hand it over to others who can't help your situation change for the better. Don't be like others who just play the "blame game" and give excuses their entire lives, change now, take control, and lead others to success as well.

Chapter 8: Getting Things DONE

One of the biggest differences that I've seen between rich and poor people, between the successful and the unsuccessful, between those who *do* and those who *don't* is the fact that the people who get things <u>done</u> in life are those people who actually do them. The other side of this equation, the poor, unsuccessful, and the non-doers are those who don't do what they say—they just talk and talk and talk about it 'till the cows come home. You will see this all over the place, especially in negative people; they never do anything because they either don't believe that they *can* do anything, or they don't think it'll work out, or whatever.

A big indicator of who this type of person, the "talk-about-it" is can be seen from a phrase that they use: "I <u>should</u>...". I *should* go to bed on time tonight. I should take out the trash the first time I'm asked. I really should start eating healthy. Truthfully, these people who say this two-word phrase really know what's good for them, but they don't have the courage to just take the first step forward, just to start that little spark that will ignite into a huge forest fire of passion, which will carry them through the rest of the actions they know they should do. Be honest with yourself.

When I was a kid, I would always have these genius ideas for companies, for innovative products—that's who I was and still am today, I'm almost finished with a patent for a revolutionary device as I write this. So I'd present these ideas to my Dad, and he'd tell me: "well you know, there's already a company out there that does this", or "well, here's what you need to know before starting that: you'd need a company name, you'd need lawyers, you'd need to source your products from somewhere, you'd need to organize the shipping, etc.". While I'm sure he was trying to be helpful, those responses really turned me off, effectively killing my ideas, because I'd get caught up in all of those details, and end up doing nothing.

Now, I understand where my Dad was coming from, that he as a father was trying to help his son and make sure that I didn't make any mistakes, but here's the thing: you actually *don't* need to write a whole business plan in order to start a business, you don't need to "set everything up" in many cases. You just need that commitment to what you're going to do, a belief in what you are offering so strong that all the details just fall to the side. With *any* idea or plan that you have, *any* dream that you want fulfilled, you have to commit first, and don't worry, you'll figure out the details later. You just need to stop thinking, stop saying "I should do it", and just DO IT. Don't get caught up in all of the details—yes, it can be beneficial to ask the advice of people who have done something similar before, but the most important thing to do whenever you get an idea is to just DO something. Take it one step at a time, and you'll figure the details out as you go along.

For example, when the founders of Google started their company, did they sketch out how they'd run their company in 20 years from then, how they would manage over 100,000 employees? No! They figured it out as they went along. In the year 1986, did Steve Jobs plan on how to market the iPod 15 years later? No, because back then it wasn't even an idea! You have to just take actions, just start doing something, and figure out the rest as you go along.

There are two HUGE concepts in this area that a lot of people get wrong, either due to their upbringing, or to how they've been influenced by society, etc. The first is that many people spend a ton of time planning, and only start doing something once they've sketched out a plan. The problem is, things always come up, and the plans usually have to be adjusted. If you follow this principle in life, I assure you that you won't go wrong in whatever you do: just <u>do something</u>, and keep on moving! If you keep on doing things, you *will* get somewhere.

Secondly, most people on this planet try to get "just enough"; they don't aim to gather that overabundance of money/possessions that is necessary in order to deal with curveballs in life. You never know when you might need an extra $4,000 in order to take care of a medical issue that just came up (or $400,000), or some extra money to remove a tree that just fell in your yard. Go for more, and *at the very least* you'll end up having "just enough".

One BIG BIG BIG reason as to why many people don't do the things that they should, don't take the first leap of action, and don't eventually succeed in life is because they have regrets. How does having regrets stop you from taking action? You see, you should NEVER regret ANYTHING that you EVER do, because if you regret one thing, who's to say you won't regret the next thing you do? Even if you did something really stupid, like got drunk and ended up accidentally breaking your best friend's arm, don't regret it, rather look at the positive; at the very least look at it as a learning experience: "now I know not to get drunk when anyone else is around" (or just don't get drunk at all, that's never helped anyone except for in the Medieval Ages when they amputated limbs—they used alcohol to numb the patients). Regrets will kill your motivation to do anything more in your life, and even when you *do* start taking action, past regrets will keep you nervous and scared that whatever you are doing, you might regret it later, which causes you not to put your full effort into what you are doing. NEVER REGRET ANYTHING. EVER. The past is meant to be learned from, not to make your life filled with fear and misery.

Speaking of fear, that's another reason why you should stop reading and listening to the news, because if it's not just negativity, then it's going to be negativity and fear together. Stories such as "this person invested in the stock market and lost EVERYTHING in just 1 day" (fear—don't invest in the stock market); "a record number of babies died this year from the flu" (fear—don't have kids right now. Hey, did they ever tell you that out of 300 Million Americans, last year's record was 101 deaths and this year it's 110? I'm not saying that because those deaths don't matter, I'm putting it into perspective that although yes, there were 110 child deaths from the flu, that was out of 300,000,000 so your chances are pretty slim, especially if you're healthy); "hikers die while hiking in Colorado after just 3 days" (fear—never go hiking. They don't ever tell you the full story, do they?). Yes, you should be aware of issues and risks such as investing pitfalls, health issues, and safety, but don't let that awareness eat you from the inside out and make you scared to do anything, because it *will* if you let it!

The best way to conquer fear is to either <u>know what you're doing</u>, or to <u>just do it</u>. Do you think Felix Baumgartner (look him up if you don't know who he is) was afraid when he parachuted from 128,000 feet above the ground? Maybe, but let me tell you, he'd have been a LOT more afraid if he didn't know what he was doing, right? The source of fear is the unknown, that's why people are scared of bugs, because they move so fast, you don't know if they're going to crawl on you, and then you don't know if they're going to bite you! People are scared of the dark, because they don't know what is in the darkness; if they knew that there was nothing inside the room, they wouldn't be as scared. And even if you don't know what's going to happen, <u>do it anyway</u>, because the longer you wait, the more afraid you become.

Why am I talking about fear right now in this book on personal development? Because it is those things that you fear that you should do, that's where you grow the most as a person in life. Conquer your fears, don't let them conquer you, and you will be known as a courageous person, someone who appears absolutely fearless, and that will gain you a tremendous amount of respect in everyone's eyes, including your own.

While we're talking about doing things in that moment of fear when you aren't sure how it's going to turn out, let's talk about two more things that will help you push through those types of things, every day: Commitment and purpose. Those are the two most powerful energies in the world, because when a person has both of them, he becomes unstoppable. Now you can only have commitment when you have a purpose; if you are committed without a purpose, that's called "motivation", something temporary which comes one day and leaves the next. You have to find a purpose other than just making money (because if you think about it, there is no purpose in money, it's just a means to an end), and then become completely committed to that purpose, and then nothing will be able to stand in your way.

Now here's the question: how do you find your purpose? I'll answer that right now, then I'll explain, and then I'll tell you the answer again, and at that time you will understand it a whole lot more: <u>don't complicate things</u>. How does that answer the question? Let me explain something first.

There is a concept, a saying in the world that "the A students teach the B students how to work for the C students, and the D students dedicate the building". What's the truth behind this ever-popular saying? It can be interpreted in many ways, but I believe that it is telling us a critical concept about how to live life. I am not going to tell you that getting good grades in school isn't important, because it is, as getting good grades teaches you discipline and gets you more knowledge and self-confidence, rather I am telling you what I am about to share with you for two reasons: 1) to tell you that even if you do/did get poor grades in school there is still hope for you to be successful, and 2) because I want to share with you how C students think, as it is super-important to adopt this way of thinking to *all* aspects of "real life".

Now, what causes the C students, the ones who were "academically challenged" or didn't like doing homework, following rules, or just didn't like school, to be so successful? People like Elon Musk, Mark Cuban, Peter Thiel, who have become known as names of financial success, what mindset did they have in order to achieve the great things that others struggled to create? I believe that it is because of 3 reasons: 1) they didn't like following rules because they think differently than everyone else and realize that it's very valuable to do so; 2) they are extremely driven to succeed, and 3) because they don't complicate things:

1) They think differently: "if you don't want to be like the 99%, don't do what the 99% do". Revolutionary products weren't created by people who have learned to think "inside the box", they were thought up by people who didn't want to "go with the flow", and instead created something that they believed in, and were therefore able to take those ideas to market with a passion.
2) They are extremely driven to succeed: I've wondered this for a very long time: why is it that you hear and read stories of people who do extraordinary things, and most of the time, if not all of the time those people started from nothing or from very rough beginnings (I mentioned this earlier)? The answer is because since they started from such a low point in their lives, they hit rock-bottom, they had to push really hard in order to get out of that pit of despair, and once they got out they kept on pushing, because that's the level of effort and

activity that they were used to using, a level of energy far above the levels that an average person deems necessary.

3) Because they don't complicate things: One of the reasons why C and D students get those grades in school is because their brains aren't as "technologically advanced" as the B students or A students. Unlike society would like us to believe, this is NOT a disadvantage; on the contrary, it's a HUGE advantage. To understand this we must first accept something as true, the basis of this book: everything in your life, from the amount of success that you will have to the amount of hardship, is determined by the way you think. If you think about how unapproachable a certain person is, the harder it will be to actually approach them, because you believe that it is difficult. If you think that something is complicated, then you will undoubtably make it more complicated than it actually is. On the converse, if you think that something complicated is actually easy, then easy it will become. Now since the A student has the mental capacity to deal with complex issues and calculations, when he is faced with problems, incidents, or pretty much

anything in life, he will tend to see it from a deeper, more complex point of view than those who aren't as mentally advanced as him. This causes him to make things in life much more complicated than they actually are. On the opposite side of the spectrum, the person with the "lower brainpower" sees life as a very uncomplicated process, and views anything that is too complicated for their brain as "too confusing" or "not necessary". For example, an A student will highly enjoy trying to find reasons (excuses) as to his behavior—why he is so lazy, why he doesn't like cheese, why he has a hard time waking up in the morning, etc., while the C student views that as unnecessary and instead just does things without all the complicated calculations.[2]

Let's return to our question: how do you find your purpose in life? The answer is: don't complicate things. We were all born with certain talents, things that we are naturally good at—for some it may be sales, for others it may be figuring out

---

[2] That's not to say that A students aren't needed—society needs intellectuals to make scientific discoveries, plan investments, etc., I am just explaining a social observation as to why it appears that so many people of "inferior mental capacity" in school appear to have more success in life than those who are "smart" in the classroom.

complex mathematical calculations. You should do some soul-searching, combined with feedback from other people, in order to figure out what you are good at, because that is naturally what you were meant to do. And don't say "well, there's no money in painting", because someone has to get paid for redoing the paint job on the Empire State Building! Don't say "well, I can never be super-rich working in construction"—the people who run these HUGE real estate development companies aren't begging on the streets, I'll tell you that! Do what you are good at, and you will figure out how to make money by solving problems in that industry with your unique skills, and maybe even how to start your own business in that space. Don't complicate things.

Another concept that I'd like to highlight in finding what your purpose is this: *create it*. I want you to live by the following quote: "Life is not about who you *are*. It's about who you are going to *be*." Don't spend a few years trying to figure out "who you are" and what you should be doing in life, rather just DO something and you'll figure it out as you go along! You don't need to know what your "thing" is, rather *pick* a thing, and commit to it! Maybe it's not the right "thing", your "thing", but at least it'll move you in the right direction in finding out what your "thing" really is!

Everything that you do, no matter what, should always be moving you forward. I like to display this hashtag frequently: #AMF. "Always be Moving Forward". I kinda hinted to this earlier when I spoke about "escapes" and said that the best escapes are things which are productive, things that move you forward. Because just like an icebreaker ship, if you are constantly in forward motion there is virtually nothing that can stop you. Once you stop doing any productive activity...that's usually when problems happen: people get bored and tired and start doing things that move them *backward* and withhold themselves from moving in the direction of success.

You know how people say "do what you like" for work? Well, don't be confused, because right when you heard that you probably said something like "but there are a lot of things that I like doing, and I'm very good at a bunch of different things as well! How do I know which one I should do?". I'll tell you this: yes, if you're normal you probably enjoy many things, don't worry about that. The people who profess that statement that you should enjoy what you do are probably enjoying what they do, but they had to get there first. And unless they were lucky, they had to do a lot of experimenting with different professions/jobs until they found the one that they enjoy.

I used to spend hours, sometimes 3 hours at a time, just thinking. I think I was just thinking about the current state of my life and how I could deal with any issues I was facing at that point in my life. Looking back, it wasn't the smartest thing to do, because thinking won't get you anywhere in life, you always have to be moving! You ever realize how much a toddler moves? They're *always* moving towards whatever goal is in their head at the present moment! Yes, I'm saying that you should act like a toddler in that regard: ALWAYS be moving towards the target that you set for yourself, and don't do things that don't help you achieve that.

For example, in school you want to get an A on a certain test, let's say it's your final. Now, there are certain things which will move you *forward*, towards doing better on the final, such as studying, eating, sleeping (normal amounts), etc. And there are certain things which will move you *further* from your goal: hanging out on the weekend, playing video games, etc. If you really want that juicy A, I'm advising you to ONLY do those things that move you towards that. Yes, you can relax, if you need it, because then you're using the relaxation to move you forward towards your goal, not as a retreat away from it.

This skill (yes, having the mentality of always moving forward *is* a skill, something that has to be practiced until it's your second nature) is invaluable in life after school as well; as the stakes get higher (doing well on a test to get into a good college vs. not doing your job and getting fired) you'll want to make sure that this *modus operandi* is ingrained within you, until everything that you do, every day, is focused on moving you closer towards your goal.

It gets easier as you go along, don't worry.

Chapter 9: Music

So you're in high school, you're forming the way you act and the way you think, you are forming your habits and escapes, what they'll be for the rest of your life (unless you expend a huge amount of time and energy later on to change them). Going forward with our theme that <u>mindset</u> determines everything, and that you *need* to stay away from all the negative things that will hold you down, constrict your mind from thinking big, and scare you into not taking action, music has a TREMENDOUS impact on the way you will think. Music is "the language of the soul", and when people say that, I, as a natural musician can attest that it is 100% true—that when a person writes a song they put certain emotions into the song that they mean to pass along to the listeners (their soul). For instance, some music can be described as "angry" (heavy metal comes to mind), some music is "energizing", and other music is just depressing, it makes you feel like you're missing something. Like I wrote earlier, your mind is affected by the things that you put into your head, and so is your attitude, therefore when you listen to music that is angry, you will find those emotions stirring up inside of you, and vice versa: when you feel angry, you may hear an angry song in your ears that encourages that emotion to express itself.

Needless to say, a lot of music that is put out into the marketplace today is filled with negative attitudes and ways of thinking, or is made (whether the artist knows it or not) to make you think lowly of yourself. You have to watch what you put into your head, as it will affect you! I very strongly suggest to cut out any and every song that has anything negative about it, even if it just doesn't make you feel good, and <u>only</u> listen to music that *does* make you feel good. Music that pumps you up and gets you excited about life! Music that inspires you to move to the next level! Music that relaxes you too, when you need it. When you begin doing this, cutting out the songs that have negative emotions and replacing them with songs that have positive ones, I guarantee you that you will see a visible change in the way you think, in the way you speak, and the way that you feel about yourself.

Let's conclude our discussion about positivity and negativity with the following short exercise: whenever you are experiencing negative thoughts you should always try to replace it with a positive thought. Right now, take out a sheet of paper and fold it in half. Now on the left side, write down every negative thought that is running through your mind. Don't start making them up, write down the way that you're thinking and feeling right now. Good! Now review what you wrote and realize how even just reading those words makes you unhappy and sad. Then, on the right side, write down those thoughts again, only in a positive light. For example, if on the left side you wrote "I won't ever find a job for the summer", then on the right side, across from the negative line write "I *will* get a summer job soon, I'm almost there, just one more resume, one more person to meet!" (it really helps to finish the positive thoughts with an exclamation point, by the way). Do that for ALL of the negative thoughts that you have on the other side of the page.

Now: rip the paper in half on the line that you folded, and throw the negative side out. Put the positive side on your bathroom mirror, or somewhere that you'll be able to see it constantly. Those are your new thoughts, and that's the way I want you to start thinking from now on—look at that paper so much that you just glance at it and immediately know everything that's written on it.

Chapter 10: It's WHO you know

There's a popular saying that I alluded to before: "It's all about *who* you know, not *what* you know" and this is sooooo true. You will never move forward in life by just staying in your house, you need to meet people! You need to meet people who will be able to get you your dream job, you need to meet people who will expose you to new concepts on how to grow and how to make more money, you need to meet people who will introduce you to other people who can move you forward. Even if you don't have a car, you can use a rideshare app such as Uber or Lyft, or you can ride a bike, or walk to a place where people are.

That's one of the most important things that you can gain out of high school—yes, getting good grades is important, as it shows people that you are intelligent and able to perform and that you are disciplined, but equally important is meeting and making friends with people who can change your life. Imagine if you went to school with Bill Gates. What a great connection to make! Maybe there's a guy in your class right now who will be the next "richest man in the world"! You have to make lasting connections right now, this is the perfect time to do it, when you guys are all in close proximity to each other every day. Build those connections, especially with people who are smarter or more motivated than you (and aren't doing anything negative or destructive) and you'll see the benefit that having good friends will give you. But you still have to get exposure to ideas and concepts through reading (and if you hate reading, listen to an audiobook), because that allows you to tap into the minds of people much older and experienced than you so that you can eat up their wisdom and gain the tools that you need to progress further in your life of success.

When you graduate, however, the saying becomes altered a little bit; instead, it goes something like this: "It's not *what* you know, it's not *who* you know, it's *who* knows *you*". In the world outside of formal education (and I use that terms because when you aren't in school anymore you should still be learning every day. It takes a lot of self-discipline, but it's worth it) you should get yourself known, put yourself out there so that people can help you further your aims in life.

Get connected with as many people as you can!

Chapter 11: The Rule of Twos

As this book is meant to help young adults (and beyond) adopt and develop the right mindset to change who you are during, and even after you exit the incubator of school, I want to conclude with a rule that I've been working on for at least 10 years, the "Rule of Twos". I pride myself in being an exceptionally aware and observant person; I have this ability to see things that others may not, and I discovered this rule of human nature by observing many different situations over many years, so I strongly believe it to be true.

Here it is: The Rule of Twos states that any and every change or trend takes place in twos: two minutes, two hours, two days, two weeks, or two situations. In addition, it also takes no more and no less than 2 times to get used to something/someone. For instance, a person will get acclimated in a new city/house/etc. after living there for 2 days, and will become fully "used to it" after living there for 2 weeks, etc. Or a most interesting observation: the next time someone uses the word "every" in a sentence, such as "every person I've seen today is wearing an orange hat", ask them "who did you see" and most of the time they'll only be able to name...you guessed it, 2 people off the top of their head, because after seeing 2 people do something consistent, that sets the trend in the observer's eyes.

Try it today!

We also know that "3rd time is the charm", because the first two times the person throwing the darts, swinging the bat or throwing the ball was just getting used to the motion; his body and mind needed 2 times doing the same thing to adapt to the change, to the new moves. The 3rd time indicates consistency.

This rule is especially critical when it comes to personal growth, because change really only happens in twos, and the 3rd time is when it's confirmed, when it's solid and consistent.

That's what you have to do with the information in this book: yes, you may have a shift in your mindset while you are reading it and shortly thereafter as well, but you'll know *for sure* that you've made a definite change when you still have that mindset in 2 weeks from now. And of course, you have to go through this book again, because then you'll get used to the ideas contained within, and you'll become super-comfortable with applying them to your life, as well as pick up on certain points that you didn't necessarily pick up the first time around.

Know that you WILL change the world! Keep #AMF!

Have Ben speak at your school or event!

Email: hirebentospeak@gmail.com!

Made in the USA
Monee, IL
02 October 2020